③ TOPIC: HUMILITY

DATE COMPLETED

Humility is simply the ability to focus on things other than yourself. Humility means recognizing others and not making life all about you. Humility is understanding where strength comes from and being willing to give others credit. Humility means listening well and responding to those who have authority in your life. Believe it or not, humility is a position of great strength and power. When you are humble, that simply means that you are putting yourself in a position of a servant, and you are doing it by choice. Sometimes people are humble because they choose to be, and sometimes people are humbled because they are forced to be. The greatest way to live humbly is to do so by choice. Choosing to be humble will put you in position to walk in true power. How do you treat others? Are you considerate of others in the choices that you make?

MY THOUGHTS:

⇨ UPDATE YOUR MAPS

④ TOPIC: INFLUENCE

DATE COMPLETED

Influence is a key part of leadership. Influence means that what you say and what you do causes others to want to say and do those things as well. It also means that others are watching you and wanting, in some way, to be like you. Influence means that you are having an effect on how others act, do their work, and even choices that they make. A great example of how influence works is if you were to roll a ball across your floor. If that ball were to run into a chair and bounce in a new direction, we would say that the chair INFLUENCED the direction of the ball. Influence is leadership and leadership is influence. Leaders greatly influence the lives of those they lead. Growing in influence means being a good example for others and following good examples as well.

MY THOUGHTS:

⇨ UPDATE YOUR MAPS

KUEST.org

(5) TOPIC: **SUCCESS**

DATE COMPLETED

Success happens when you set a goal and reach that goal. Success means that you started out with a clear idea about the thing you wanted to achieve. It means that along the way, you endured when things were tough, that you used wisdom, and that you didn't let anything influence you to give up. Success doesn't always mean that you win, but it means that you always finish strong, grow and refuse to quit. Success helps you to be more able to help others. Success takes work and will mean making some tough decisions about the things you want to do. Success is something you can enjoy in life. In fact, if you will put your mind to it, you can succeed very often in life. Even when it seems like things are not going to work out, you can still find a way to succeed. What are some things you have succeeded at doing?

MY THOUGHTS:

⇨ UPDATE YOUR MAPS

KUEST.org

KUEST:ROCKET
LEADERSHIP SERIES

Personal Growth MAPS

This workbook will help you become stronger at setting goals, measuring your progress and adjusting your course toward success. This is how to get started with your Personal Growth MAPs.

STEP 1: **SET YOUR MAPS |** Have a parent or older sibling or friend help you set your goals in each of the 5 MAPS located in the back of this resource. You will find step-by-step instructions for setting your goals and action items. Additional video resources are also available for parents and/or guardians on our webasite, www.KUEST.org, to help you make the most of this step.

STEP 2: **START YOUR COURSE |** Once you have your MAPs prepared, you can begin your weekly lessons as outlined below.

WEEK 1 | WISDOM [LESSON 1]

Read your "WISDOM" Lesson, then complete ALL of your MAPs updates.

WEEK 2 | ENDURANCE [LESSON 2]

Read your "ENDURANCE" Lesson, then complete ALL of your MAPs updates.

WEEK 3 | HUMILITY [LESSON 3]

Read your "HUMILITY" Lesson, then complete ALL of your MAPs updates.

WEEK 4 | INFLUENCE [LESSON 4]

Read your "INFLUENCE" Lesson, then complete ALL of your MAPs updates.

WEEK 5 | SUCCESS [LESSON 5]

Read your "SUCCESS" Lesson, then complete ALL of your MAPs updates.

Follow this pattern until you have completed all 30 lessons.

STEP 3: **FINISH STRONG |** Over the course of the year, you will track your growth on your MAPs. Once you have reached the end of this course, you will be able to look back and see your progress in each of these areas.

KUEST.org

① **TOPIC: WISDOM**

DATE COMPLETED ⬭

Wisdom is an important part of success. Wisdom means knowing the right thing to do at the right time in the right way to get the right results. For example, you might know that salt can make food taste better. So you might think, *"I will pour a whole lot of salt on my mashed potatoes."* You might even dump everything in the salt shaker on your potatoes. That would be a bad idea. Too much salt tastes terrible, and can also be bad for your health. You might also think, *"If salt can make my food taste better, then I am going to put salt on my cereal."* That would also be a bad idea. Salt is not sweet, and on most sweet food, salt is a bad idea. Wisdom would help you use salt for the right purpose on the right food in the right amount to get the right results. Is there an area of your life where you think you could use some wisdom?

MY THOUGHTS:

⇨ **UPDATE YOUR MAPS**

② **TOPIC: ENDURANCE**

DATE COMPLETED ⬭

Having endurance means that you are able to finish what you start. If you were to start a race and not finish, would you win? If you want to be successful in life, you have to learn to stick with something until it is completed. That means you are going to have to build your endurance. Endurance is especially important when you are trying to do something that is difficult or boring. When something is hard to do, you might want to stop and just walk away. When something is boring, you might want to do something more exciting or fun. If you are going to enjoy success in life, you must build your endurance. Are there areas of your life where you think you could use more endurance? What are you going to do to build your endurance in that area?

MY THOUGHTS:

⇨ **UPDATE YOUR MAPS**

KUEST.org

KUEST:ROCKET
LEADERSHIP SERIES

(6) TOPIC: WISDOM

DATE COMPLETED

Sometimes, when you face a problem, you might feel like there are only one or two options. For example, you might need a certain amount of money to buy something you really want. You might think, "I will ask my parents." or "I will sell something I have." If those two things do not work out, you might think about giving up. However, there are other things you might be able to do to get the money you need. For example, doing additional chores or earning the money through doing odd-jobs around your neighborhood, or you might even think about using the money you have to buy some items you can sell for a greater price. When you have wisdom, you have options. In fact, with wisdom, your options can almost be unlimited. What are some areas in which you may have been limiting yourself? How can wisdom help you find more options?

MY THOUGHTS:

(7) TOPIC: ENDURANCE

DATE COMPLETED

Endurance leads to success. There are times when you might try to do something over and over again and fail every time. No matter how hard you try, it just seems like you can never succeed. The truth is, every time you make an attempt, you are getting stronger and growing in wisdom. Every time you try, you gain a little more knowledge about how to get it done. Thomas Edison failed nearly 1,000 times to invent the lightbulb. Once he was asked how he felt about failing so many times. His reply was something like, "I haven't failed 1,000 times, I just know 1,000 ways to not make a lightbulb." Endurance means never giving up. If you will keep going, learning and getting stronger and wiser, endurance will lead us to success. Are you tempted to give up? What can you do to keep going?

MY THOUGHTS:

KUEST.org

⑧ **TOPIC: HUMILITY**

DATE COMPLETED

Humility brings grace. Grace is getting what you don't deserve. Can you imagine driving on a highway that was exactly the width of your car with steep dropoffs on each side? Even the slightest mistake could send you flying off those cliffs. That would be bad. Thank goodness there is room outside the white lines on highways to help us when we swerve a little. This is exactly what grace is like. Grace helps us when we are a little out of control and can keep us from getting into trouble. When we are humble, admit our mistakes, sincerely apologize and work to change our actions, we are more likely to receive grace. In other words, humility will help keep us on the right path. What are some areas in which you could be quicker to admit mistakes and make things right?

MY THOUGHTS:

⑨ **TOPIC: INFLUENCE**

DATE COMPLETED

Who is influencing you? This is one of the most important questions you can ask. Who in your life is influencing the way you think, act and make decisions? You can often see who influences you the most by paying attention to how you act. Most likely you will see that some of the habits you have and the choices you make will be a lot like the people who influence your life. You might even dress like them, play the same sport they play and even talk the way they talk. It may be a sports star, someone in your family or just a close friend. Choosing who you allow to influence your life is a very important decision. You want to choose people who are honest, fair, humble, kind and so on to be your influencers. When you look at your life, who are the biggest influences on you?

MY THOUGHTS:

KUEST.org

KUEST:ROCKET
LEADERSHIP SERIES

(10) **TOPIC: SUCCESS**

DATE COMPLETED

Success takes work. Noone has ever succeeded by doing nothing. Even when success comes easily, it still takes effort. Many times, being successful is going to take very hard work. It might even mean working hard for a very long time to get to the goal you have set for youself. Learning to work hard will make it much more likely that you will enjoy success. Work is good and makes you stronger. Using your mind, your muscles, your patience and attention to detail are all great ways to grow. The more you have success in the things you do, the more you will want to do. When your goals get bigger, so will the effort it takes to achieve those goals. Knowing now that success takes work means you can work to grow yourself for greater success. What are some dreams you have that you know will take hard work?

MY THOUGHTS:

UPDATE YOUR MAPS

KUEST.org

(11) **TOPIC: WISDOM**

DATE COMPLETED ⬭

One of the best ways to grow in wisdom is to learn to ask good questions. The truth is that everything you need to know is already around you. Whether it is in a book, online or from someone that you know, wisdom is never more than a few questions away. If we do not ask questions, we may never find the best answer. When you are trying to figure out a problem, or are just curious about something, asking questions is the best way to find the answers you need. Asking questions is also a great way to build up a lot of knowledge and wisdom. For example, if you tried to build something, you might spend a lot of time learning to use tools on your own. Or you could find someone you know that has building experience and ask them to teach you the best way. That is wisdom. What questions can you ask to help you solve a problem you are facing?

MY THOUGHTS:

⇨ **UPDATE YOUR MAPS**

(12) **TOPIC: ENDURANCE**

DATE COMPLETED ⬭

Endurance helps us grow in wisdom. When we stick with our goals and refuse to give up, we become learning sponges. There is a ton of knowledge to be gained from endurance. Every time you ride your bike, sing a song, play a sport, work on your schoolwork and so on, you are growing not only in endurance but in wisdom. You know more than ever about riding your bike. You become an even stronger teammate and skilled in your position on the team. You know more about a certain subject than ever, all because you refuse to give up and stick with your goals until you succeed. Endurance is a very powerful tool for life. It not only helps you get the job done, it can make you smarter in the process. What do you know more about today because you decided to not give up?

MY THOUGHTS:

⇨ **UPDATE YOUR MAPS**

KUEST.org

KUEST:ROCKET
LEADERSHIP SERIES

(13) TOPIC: HUMILITY

DATE COMPLETED

Humility helps us care more about others. A person who is humble understands that they are not perfect. They know that sometimes they make mistakes. They also know that others are not perfect and that sometimes others make mistakes. When you recognize that others are not perfect, and that you are not perfect either, it will help you learn to care about others more. You will be more willing to forgive the things that others do because you realize that sometimes you also make mistakes. Humility will also help you be more compassionate toward others. When you see someone hurting, or in need, compassion causes you to feel the desire to help. Growing in humility will cause you to understand the needs of others in a greater way. Are there some ways in which you can be more helpful to those around you?

MY THOUGHTS:

(14) TOPIC: INFLUENCE

DATE COMPLETED

Whom are you influencing? Just as you are influenced by others, others are influenced by you. In fact, you may not even be aware that others are watching you and are influenced by your life. If you pay attention, you may start to notice that some of your freinds choose the same things you choose, or act the way you act, or think that you are awesome and just want to be like you. Sometimes this can mean that you are having a great influence on their lives. The truth is, even when you are not aware, you are influencing others. Choosing to be a positive influence is an important part of being a great leader. Watching what you say, how you act and the choices you make will help you to be a powerful influence in the lives of others. What are some ways you positively influence others?

MY THOUGHTS:

KUEST.org

KUEST:ROCKET
LEADERSHIP SERIES

(15) TOPIC: **SUCCESS**

Success is a constant pursuit. When you are working toward a goal, say, a certain score on a test, or improving in some skill, you have to keep working toward that goal on a constant basis. Often, there are things you have to do daily if you want to succeed. For example, if you only studied math in the first grade and then never studied it again, it would be impossible to pass your math test in the 12th grade. In order to graduate from school, you have to work on math every day throughout the school year. You may miss a day here or there, but being steady in your studies is what will help you graduate when you are older. This is true for everything you are going after in life. Singing, sports, art, business, health, money; you name it! If you want to succeed, you must keep pursuing. Are there goals you need to pursue more often?

MY THOUGHTS:

UPDATE YOUR MAPS

KUEST.org

(16) TOPIC: WISDOM

Wisdom can help us avoid a bad situation. There is an old saying that goes something like this: "Sometimes wisdom is better than bravery." What that means is that sometimes it is better to avoid a situation than it is to try to do something about it. For example, maybe your little brother or a younger friend dropped their favorite ball into a storm sewer. You might be tempted to try to climb down into the storm sewer to rescue their favorite ball. That would be brave! But it might not be wise. There is a lot of danger in some situations and we often have to use wisdom before we just jump right into doing some things. Wisdom would be to ask an adult, or to maybe offer one of your favorite balls as a replacement. Wisdom will help us avoid bad situations. Are there some difficult moments you are facing for which you could use some wisdom?

MY THOUGHTS:

(17) TOPIC: ENDURANCE

Endurance will build your confidence. Maybe there are some areas of your life in which you lack confidence. Maybe you think you are not good enough to do some of the things you want to do. Maybe you struggle in certain subjects or in certain activities with your friends. Sometimes, a lack of confidence in an area can cause us to want to give up. However, if we can use our endurance muscle and stick with it, it can help us grow in confidence. For example, you may not be able to run a whole mile today, and so you are tempted to say, "I am a bad runner and will never be able to run a mile." If you let that cause you to give up, you will never reach that goal. But if you stick with it and improve just a little bit each day, soon you will confidently run a mile with no problem. In what area of your life might endurance help to build your confidence?

MY THOUGHTS:

KUEST.org

KUEST:ROCKET
LEADERSHIP SERIES

(18) TOPIC: **HUMILITY**

DATE COMPLETED ⬭

Humility is not proud. When you do something really cool, you probably want others to notice. That's ok because we all want to be noticed and recognized by those we love the most. However, sometimes you might be tempted to make everyone recognize how great you think you are by bragging or comparing yourself to others. You might say, "Look at what I did! Isn't it great?" Or you might even say to a friend, "Mine is better than yours!" When you do these things, you are not acting in humility, but in pride. Being proud is the opposite of being humble. Pride is often very self-centered, while humility is about building others up. It is ok to want to be recognized for something you have accomplished; it is not ok to force others to recognize you. Are there times when you try to make others notice you? What can you do to be humble in those moments?

MY THOUGHTS:

⇨ UPDATE YOUR MAPS

(19) TOPIC: **INFLUENCE**

DATE COMPLETED ⬭

When you have influence, others want to know what you think. The more you grow in wisdom and the more you do in life, the more influence you will have. When others ask you to share your thoughts and ideas, that is influence. What you tell them may make a big difference in how they think or the choices they make. Making solid choices, working hard and having a positive attitude will help you get the most out of life. What you learn from the way you live may be just the thing someone else needs to help them succeed. That is influence. How are the choices you are making today helping you be a person of influence?

MY THOUGHTS:

⇨ UPDATE YOUR MAPS

KUEST.org

KUEST:ROCKET
LEADERSHIP SERIES

(20) **TOPIC: SUCCESS**

DATE COMPLETED (   )

Success is a blessing. You know that success is something that you can work toward. You also know that success takes being consistent at doing the things you know you need to do. When you work hard, stick with it, keep your eye on the goal and finally achieve success, it is a blessing. Sure, you have earned a part of that success. It is the result of your focus and effort. It is also important to remember that success can be temporary. For example, scoring a 100 on your math test does not mean that you will automatically score 100 the next time. Be sure to stop and be thankful for scoring well on your test. When we see success as a blessing, we will not take it for granted. We will appreciate it and enjoy it even more. What are some ways that you like to celebrate a success?

MY THOUGHTS:

⇨ UPDATE YOUR MAPS

KUEST.org

KUEST:ROCKET
LEADERSHIP SERIES

(21) TOPIC: **WISDOM**

DATE COMPLETED

Wisdom can help us be more effective. There is an old phrase that says, "Sharpen the axe!" What does that mean? Can you imagine trying to cut down a tree with a dull axe? Maybe the axe is so dull that it wouldn't even cut a tomato! You could swing that axe at that tree for days and never cut it down. Rather than just trying to swing harder and harder, this old phrase, "Sharpen the axe," means to use wisdom. Even though working hard is an important part of success, working harder is not always the answer. Sometimes the answer is "Working smarter!" This is what it means to "Sharpen the axe." Wisdom will help you find the best way to accomplish your task. Often it will mean hard work, but it will always mean working our hardest in the smartest way possible. What are some things that you find hard to do? Is there a smarter way to do them?

MY THOUGHTS:

⇨ UPDATE YOUR MAPS

(22) TOPIC: **ENDURANCE**

DATE COMPLETED

Endurance will expand your view of life. Sometimes your view of life can be limited by the things that limit you. Maybe you feel a subject is too difficult and you think, "Why do I need to study this anyway?" If you did not push through the difficulty, you might stop trying and only gain a small part of the knowledge you could have. This would limit your view of what is possible in life. When you choose to say, "I'm going to dig in and get this done!" you open yourself up to greater possibilities and that will expand your view of life. Now, instead of just giving up when something is hard, you know you can take on much more difficult moments and succeed! You are not a quitter, you are a winner! How can you allow endurance to expand your view of life?

MY THOUGHTS:

⇨ UPDATE YOUR MAPS

KUEST.org

KUEST:ROCKET
LEADERSHIP SERIES

(23) TOPIC: HUMILITY

DATE COMPLETED

Humility is not selfish. Sometimes it is hard to let others have their way. When you are playing games, choosing food or wanting to spend time in your room alone, it can be difficult to allow others to particiapte or allow others to choose what to do. It is ok to have alone time. it is ok to get to choose for yourself. It is also ok to allow others to choose and to include them. If everyone allows every-one to have a turn then everyone gets a turn. But if nobody allows anybody to have a turn then nobody gets a turn. Humility means being focused on others even more than your own desires. It means sharing, making room for others and being willing to not get your own way all the time. How can you make more room for what others want in your life?

MY THOUGHTS:

UPDATE YOUR MAPS

(24) TOPIC: INFLUENCE

DATE COMPLETED

Choosing to listen to the right voices in your life is how you choose the right influences. Whether you are listening to music, watching movies, reading books or hanging out with friends, you are being influenced by the voices that you hear. You are influenced by the words to the songs you hear, the stories and sugges-tions from your friends, the content of the movies or shows you watch and the subjects of the books you read. All of these can have a big and powerful influ-ence in your attitude, your choices and your life. The good news is that, for the most part, you get to choose. You can choose the music, the movies and even your friends. You can choose the voices that get to influence your life. Choose wisely! Choose positive, empowering and encouraging voices! Are there voices you need to choose to not allow to be an influence in your life?

MY THOUGHTS:

UPDATE YOUR MAPS

KUEST.org

(25) **TOPIC: SUCCESS**

DATE COMPLETED

Success is important, but it is not the most important thing. Have you ever been so focused on winning that you treated others meanly? Have you ever cried about losing? Have you ever found yourself upset at someone else because they did better than you? Have you ever been jealous because someone else was praised for their achievement while you were not? If you have felt any of these things, you are not alone. All of us deal with these feelings at some time. The important thing to remember is this: While it is good to work at being your best and going after success, there is more to a good life. The way we show love to others, our willingness to help, being kind and encouraging are all more important than winning. The good news is, you can do both. Go after success AND treat others with love and respect. How well do you do this?

MY THOUGHTS:

UPDATE YOUR MAPS

KUEST.org

KUEST:ROCKET
LEADERSHIP SERIES

(26) TOPIC: **WISDOM**

DATE COMPLETED

Wisdom allows us to help others. As you grow in wisdom, you will find that others will depend on you to help them find the best, smartest, most effective way to get stuff done. When you have wisdom - knowing the right thing to do at the right time in the right way to get the right results - you become a valuable resource for others. Just like the people around you are helping you, when you have wisdom, you become someone that others can trust to help them. When you use your wisdom to help others, your wisdom is growing as well. You will learn what works and what does not work. You will find even greater wisdom by using what you have to help others. Wisdom is an important part of success. You should always work hard to grow your wisdom. Who do you know that could use some wisdom today?

MY THOUGHTS:

(27) TOPIC: **ENDURANCE**

DATE COMPLETED

Endurance will build your strength. There will be times when you are given the chance to take the easy way out. Others may make offers that you know are not right. You will likely face moments when relationships get hard, when you don't have all the money you need, or even face a physical challenge. In these moments, you want to be able to call on great strength to help you get through. Building up your ability to endure is a very important part of success in these moments. Finishing math, taking out the trash, running just one more lap, all of these can help you become a young leader with great endurance. Endurance will give you the strength in very challenging times to stand strong and succeed! Keep it up, you are building your endurance! How can you step up your endurance?

MY THOUGHTS:

KUEST.org

KUEST:ROCKET
LEADERSHIP SERIES

(28) TOPIC: HUMILITY

Humility leads to peace. Have you ever felt sad or left out or mad because you didn't get your way? Have you ever felt excluded because your friends didn't choose to do things the way you wanted? It is important that you work hard to be inclusive and encouraging with your friends. Sometimes we are the ones who feel the hurt of being left out. Growing in humility - the willingness to put others first - will help you be at peace even when you feel things did not go your way. If you already let others go first, then when others act selfishly, it will not matter as much. Rather than being hurt or upset, you might even find that you encourage them to act more humbly themselves. There is peace in being humble. That peace comes from knowing you have all that you need to enjoy success. How can you include others more?

MY THOUGHTS:

(29) TOPIC: INFLUENCE

Good influences will keep you headed in the right direction. Remember the ball we talked about rolling across your floor in week 4? When that ball hit the chair, it moved in a different direction. Maybe that was the wrong direction. Maybe it was the right direction. It all depends on where YOU wanted the ball to go. In the same way, you have the ability to choose your direction in life. You can choose to work hard, be a good friend and go after success. You can choose to allow things in life to influence you in the right direction. When something tries to stop your progress, find a way around it. If a voice in your life is influencing you the wrong way, choose not to listen! Choose to follow those influences that keep you moving in the right direction. What is influencing you in the right way?

MY THOUGHTS:

KUEST.org

(30) TOPIC: SUCCESS

DATE COMPLETED

Success is just the beginning. If you have ever had a goal, worked hard and achieved that goal, then you know what it feels like to be done! What a great feeling that is! When you have finished your schoolwork for the day...DONE! When you finished your chores for the week...DONE! When your room is cleaned or practice is over...DONE! Success is a great feeling. But success is not the end, it is just the beginning. For the rest of your life you will be setting goals, working hard and enjoying success. Every time you cross a finish line of some kind, you will get to celebrate and take a deep breath. Then it is off to the next goal! The great thing is that, for you, life is going to be filled with many successes. Enjoy them all! Success is not the end, it is just the beginning! What are you looking forward to in your future?

MY THOUGHTS:

⇨ UPDATE YOUR MAPS

KUEST.org

BUILD YOUR SUCCESS M.A.P.

DESTINATION: Where would you like for your ROCKET to land? Describe your goal for growing in SUCCESS:

TOPIC: (ex: "Work hard to complete my chores at home").

DESCRIBE YOUR DESTINATION: (ex: "I will complete all my chores without being reminded"). Be as detailed as possible.

SET YOUR COURSE

What are the things you need to do every week in order to grow so you can reach your goal in this area? (ex: "I will time myself, try to focus and get my work done more quickly each week while still doing an excellent job"). Please list no more than 3.

FOLLOW YOUR M.A.P.

MEASURE

When you do your task for the week, color in a small circle. If you do not do your task, put an X through a small circle. Once all circles are filled in or have an X, do the next measurement.

ADJUST

Are there some things you need to do differently? (ex: "Turn off the TV until all my chores are done"). Write your new adjustments here.

PROGRESS

Now that you have made some adjustments, follow your updated plan. Then show your completed new weekly tasks on the circles as before.

On a scale between 1-10, rate yourself compared to the goal you have set. 1 = not close, 10 = goal accomplished. Write the date you put down this score.

Measurement Date

On a scale between 1-10, rate yourself compared to the goal you have set. 1 = not close, 10 = goal accomplished. Write the date you put down this score.

Measurement Date

On a scale between 1-10, rate yourself compared to the goal you have set. 1 = not close, 10 = goal accomplished. Write the date you put down this score.

Measurement Date

MEASUREMENT #1

1	2	3	4	5	6
7	8	9	10	11	12
13	14	15	16	17	18

1	2	3	4	5	6
7	8	9	10	11	12
13	14	15	16	17	18

1	2	3	4	5	6
7	8	9	10	11	12
13	14	15	16	17	18

MEASUREMENT #2

MEASUREMENT #3

19	20	21	22	23	24
25	26	27	28	29	30
31	32	33	34	35	36

19	20	21	22	23	24
25	26	27	28	29	30
31	32	33	34	35	36

19	20	21	22	23	24
25	26	27	28	29	30
31	32	33	34	35	36

MAKE YOUR WISDOM M.A.P.

© copyright 2016, Current Family, Inc.

DESTINATION: Where would you like for your ROCKET to land? Describe your goal for growing in WISDOM:

TOPIC: (ex: "I want to use my money more wisely").

DESCRIBE YOUR DESTINATION: (ex: "I want to save $50 and open my own savings account"). Be as detailed as possible.

SET YOUR COURSE

What are the things you need to do every week in order to grow in wisdom for your goal? (ex: "I will read an article on saving money every week"). Please list no more than 3.

FOLLOW YOUR M.A.P.

On a scale between 1-10, how much do you know about this topic right now? 1=nothing, 10 =everything. Write the date you put down this score.

Measurement Date

Do you know more or the same? Have you grown in this area since you began? What is your number now?

Measurement Date

Now how much do you know about this topic? Have you grown in wisdom since your last score?

Measurement Date

MEASURE

When you do your task for the week, color in a small circle. If you do not do your task, put an X through a small circle. Once all circles are filled in or have an X, do the next measurement.

ADJUST

Are there some things you need to do differently? (ex: "Stop spending my money on candy"). Write your new adjustments here.

PROGRESS

Now that you have made some adjustments, follow your updated plan. Then show your completed new weekly tasks on the circles as before.

MEASUREMENT #1

1	2	3	4	5	6
7	8	9	10	11	12
13	14	15	16	17	18

1	2	3	4	5	6
7	8	9	10	11	12
13	14	15	16	17	18

1	2	3	4	5	6
7	8	9	10	11	12
13	14	15	16	17	18

MEASUREMENT #2

MEASUREMENT # 3

19	20	21	22	23	24
25	26	27	28	29	30
31	32	33	34	35	36

19	20	21	22	23	24
25	26	27	28	29	30
31	32	33	34	35	36

19	20	21	22	23	24
25	26	27	28	29	30
31	32	33	34	35	36

CREATE YOUR ENDURANCE M.A.P.

© copyright 2016, Current Family, Inc.

DESTINATION: Where would you like for your ROCKET to land? Describe your goal for growing in STATURE:

TOPIC: (ex: "Be a better runner").

DESCRIBE YOUR DESTINATION: (ex: "By the end of summer, I want to be able to run a whole lap around my neighborhood without stopping"). Be as detailed as possible.

SET YOUR COURSE

What are the things you need to do every week in order to grow in the area of this topic? (ex: "I need to run a little bit every day and add to how far I run every week.") Please list no more than 3.

FOLLOW YOUR M.A.P.

On a scale from 1 - 10, measure your endurance. 1 = very little, 10 = maximum to your goal. Write the date you put down this score.

On a scale from 1 - 10, measure your endurance. 1=very little, 10 = maximum to your goal. Write the date you put down this score.

On a scale from 1 - 10, measure your endurance. 1=very little, 10 = maximum to your goal. Write the date you put down this score.

MEASURE
When you do your task for the week, color in a small circle. If you do not do your task, put an X through a small circle. Once all circles are filled in or have an X, do the next measurement.

ADJUST
Are there some things you need to do differently? (ex: "Run a little slower and drink more water.") Write your new adjustments here.

PROGRESS
Now that you have made some adjustments, follow your updated plan. Then show your completed new weekly tasks on the circles as before.

Measurement Date

MEASUREMENT #1
1 2 3 4 5 6
7 8 9 10 11 12
13 14 15 16 17 18

1 2 3 4 5 6
7 8 9 10 11 12
13 14 15 16 17 18

1 2 3 4 5 6
7 8 9 10 11 12
13 14 15 16 17 18

Measurement Date

MEASUREMENT #2

Measurement Date

MEASUREMENT # 3
19 20 21 22 23 24
25 26 27 28 29 30
31 32 33 34 35 36

19 20 21 22 23 24
25 26 27 28 29 30
31 32 33 34 35 36

19 20 21 22 23 24
25 26 27 28 29 30
31 32 33 34 35 36

DESIGN YOUR HUMILITY M.A.P.

© copyright 2016, Current Family, Inc.

DESTINATION: Where would you like for your ROCKET to land? Describe your goal for growing in HUMILITY:

TOPIC: (ex: "How to be more kind").

DESCRIBE YOUR DESTINATION: (ex: "I want to learn how to be more kind to my friends, to share better and to say things that make my friends feel good about themselves"). Be as detailed as possible.

FOLLOW YOUR M.A.P.

On a scale between 1-10, rate yourself compared to the goal you have set. 1 = not close, 10 = goal accomplished. Write the date you put down this score.

On a scale between 1-10, rate yourself compared to the goal you have set. 1 = not close, 10 = goal accomplished. Write the date you put down this score.

On a scale between 1-10, rate yourself compared to the goal you have set. 1 = not close, 10 = goal accomplished. Write the date you put down this score.

Measurement Date

Measurement Date

Measurement Date

MEASURE

When you do your task for the week, color in a small circle. If you do not do your task, put an X through a small circle. Once all circles are filled in or have an X, do the next measurement.

ADJUST

Are there some things you need to do differently? (ex: "Give an even better effort when helping others"). Write your new adjustments here.

PROGRESS

Now that you have made some adjustments, follow your updated plan. Then show your completed new weekly tasks on the circles as before.

MEASUREMENT #1

1	2	3	4	5	6
7	8	9	10	11	12
13	14	15	16	17	18

1	2	3	4	5	6
7	8	9	10	11	12
13	14	15	16	17	18

1	2	3	4	5	6
7	8	9	10	11	12
13	14	15	16	17	18

MEASUREMENT #2

MEASUREMENT #3

19	20	21	22	23	24
25	26	27	28	29	30
31	32	33	34	35	36

19	20	21	22	23	24
25	26	27	28	29	30
31	32	33	34	35	36

19	20	21	22	23	24
25	26	27	28	29	30
31	32	33	34	35	36

SET YOUR COURSE

What are the things you need to do every week in order to grow so that you can reach your goal for this topic? (ex: "Every week I will choose a friend to help and give my best to do what they need done"). Please list no more than 3.

DEVELOP YOUR INFLUENCE M.A.P.

DESTINATION: Where would you like for your ROCKET to land? Describe your goal for growing in INFLUENCE:

TOPIC: (ex: "Be a positive role model." or "Be confident to always do the right thing").

DESCRIBE YOUR DESTINATION: (ex: "I want to learn how to be the kind of person that can help my friends make good choices." or "I will listen to my conscience more than peer pressure"). Be as detailed as possible.

FOLLOW YOUR M.A.P.

On a scale between 1-10, rate yourself compared to the goal you have set. 1 = not close, 10 = goal accomplished. Write the date you put down this score.

Measurement Date

MEASURE
When you do your task for the week, color in a small circle. If you do not do your task, put an X through a small circle. Once all circles are filled in or have an X, do the next measurement.

MEASUREMENT #1

1	2	3	4	5	6
7	8	9	10	11	12
13	14	15	16	17	18

1	2	3	4	5	6
7	8	9	10	11	12
13	14	15	16	17	18

1	2	3	4	5	6
7	8	9	10	11	12
13	14	15	16	17	18

On a scale between 1-10, rate yourself compared to the goal you have set. 1 = not close, 10 = goal accomplished. Write the date you put down this score.

Measurement Date

ADJUST
Are there some things you need to do differently? (ex: "I will not be afraid to share what I know is right.") Write your new adjustments here.

MEASUREMENT #2

On a scale between 1-10, rate yourself compared to the goal you have set. 1 = not close, 10 = goal accomplished. Write the date you put down this score.

Measurement Date

PROGRESS
Now that you have made some adjustments, follow your updated plan. Then show your completed new weekly tasks on the circles as before.

MEASUREMENT # 3

19	20	21	22	23	24
25	26	27	28	29	30
31	32	33	34	35	36

19	20	21	22	23	24
25	26	27	28	29	30
31	32	33	34	35	36

19	20	21	22	23	24
25	26	27	28	29	30
31	32	33	34	35	36

SET YOUR COURSE

What are the things you need to do every week in order to grow so that you can reach your goals for this topic? (ex: "I will watch for an opportunity every week to encourage a friend to do the right thing"). Please list no more than 3.

www.ingramcontent.com/pod-product-compliance
Lightning Source LLC
Chambersburg PA
CBHW061059090426
42742CB00002B/91